ST. MICHAEL'S SCHOOL,
BRIDGEPORT, CONN.

ROBERT FULTON
AND THE STEAMBOAT

ST. MICHAEL'S SCHOOL,
BRIDGEPORT, CONN.

ST. MICHAEL'S SCHOOL,
BRIDGEPORT, CONN.

B
F

ROBERT FULTON

AND THE

STEAMBOAT

———— ★ ————

by RALPH NADING HILL

Illustrated by LEE J. AMES

Landmark BOOKS

RANDOM HOUSE · NEW YORK

IMMACULATA COLLEGE
HAMBURG, NEW YORK

10,434

Copyright *1954* by Ralph Nading Hill

All rights reserved under International
and Pan-American Copyright Conventions

Published in New York by Random House, Inc.
and simultaneously in Toronto, Canada, by
Random House of Canada, Ltd.

Library of Congress Catalog Card Number: *54-7020*
Manufactured in the U.S.A.

For George, Clark and Dolly;
Mary, Anne and Jimmy

CONTENTS

ROBERT FULTON
AND THE STEAMBOAT

1

THE DAYDREAMER

WHEN ROBERT FULTON WAS A SCHOOLBOY OF nine, there was as yet no United States. But the feeling against England was running strong and bitter throughout the thirteen colonies. He could hardly have failed to hear or understand the shouts of "Liberty!" that were ringing through the streets, for it was 1774, only one year before the first shot of the Revolution was fired.

"Fulton!" boomed the voice of the teacher as he took up his switch. Robert's eyes went quickly back to his desk, his ears turning a deep scarlet as laughter ran through the classroom. Although he was now looking at his book, he was not making any sense out of its pages. His mind was wandering.

He was not an attentive student in his early years, and on many occasions he went home bearing the marks of the teacher's switch. "My head is so full of my own notions," he complained to his mother, "that there is no room to store up the contents of dusty books."

Outside of school as time went on, his friends called him "Quicksilver Bob" because he was always making experiments with that strange element—what experiments we do not know. And it is surely a fact that he spent much of his spare time around the shops of Isch and Messersmith, who were making and repairing guns for the Colonial troops.

What could be more exciting for a boy interested in the wonders of the mechanical arts than to be the only youth allowed inside a guarded

Robert loved to watch the strong-armed black-smiths at the forge

factory where guns were being made? The fires of the forges glowed orange. Blow after blow of the strong-armed blacksmiths fell on ringing anvils. At the many workbenches craftsmen were assembling the tiny parts of the trigger mechanisms. It was this, not the schoolroom textbook, that stirred Robert's imagination. Historians say he was so observant and so clever that he frequently made suggestions and drawings that were followed by the men at the shops.

When Robert was fourteen, he became fast friends with an eighteen-year-old boy named Christopher who was an apprentice at Isch and Messersmith. They made many trips into the country around Lancaster, often with Christopher's father, Peter Gumpf, who liked to fish on Conestoga Creek. On these occasions, they boarded a flat-bottomed boat which Robert and Christopher would push with long poles from

Robert fastened paddle wheels to Peter Gumpf's boat

one fishing spot to another. This was an awkward means of locomotion at best.

On a visit to the home of his aunt in Little

Britain Township, Robert made a small model of a fishing boat with paddle wheels on each side. When he returned to Lancaster, he built a pair of wheels patterned after the ones on his model and fastened them to Peter Gumpf's boat. Two hand cranks connected the wheels. And when he and Christopher turned the cranks, the boat moved smartly forward. Henceforth, the paddle-wheel boat propelled the two boys and Peter Gumpf on their fishing trips. Years later one of Fulton's family remembered that the small model Robert had made could still be seen in the parlor of his aunt's house.

2

A HOPEFUL ARTIST

ROBERT FULTON'S EARLY LIFE WAS HARD, LIKE
that of many other great Americans. His father
was a tailor who bought a farm on the outskirts
of Lancaster, Pennsylvania, when Robert was
very small. The soil was poor, the crops were
meager and the elder Fulton lost everything he
had. He then moved his wife and three daughters
and Robert back to Lancaster. There he once
again took up his trade as a tailor. He died three
years later, and the family had to struggle along
in poverty until Robert became old enough to
earn a living for his mother and three older sisters.

Robert had another talent besides that of being handy with tools and mechanical objects; he liked to paint and was good at it. In school one day a classmate had brought in some colors mixed in shells. Watching with fascination as his friend applied the bright colors to paper and blended them into a picture, Robert asked: "Would you lend me some of those colors? I'd like to try to paint."

"Have you ever painted before?"

"No."

"Here," said his friend taking a little of each color from the different shells. "You won't find it easy to do."

Thanking his friend, Robert studied the colors—bright red, blue and green. They seemed almost too precious to waste on paper. Then he began to paint, letting his imagination guide his brush. Before very long he had a picture which was so good that it astonished not only the friend who had loaned him the colors, but his other classmates as well. "Look what Robert did," they shouted, for they could not believe he had never painted before.

"Here," said his friend at length. "Take all my colors. If you can paint like that without any practice, you ought to have them." Overjoyed, Robert gathered up the colors as if they were gold, took them home, and then began to paint in earnest. Soon his pictures began to draw the attention of the townspeople, who agreed that he had remarkable talent. As the months passed, he worked along diligently, gaining experience that proved to be of great value in the years ahead.

Perhaps it isn't strange that the boy should have taken up his brush and paints at the very time that Benjamin West, a famous portrait painter and friend of Robert's father, was also living in Lancaster. Perhaps the boy's desire to be an artist was an attempt to imitate West, who was so much admired by his fellow citizens of Pennsylvania.

At any rate, while still very young, Fulton began painting trade signs to be hung outside the local shops and thus earned a little money to help support his family. Later, while still in his teens, he became the apprentice of Jeremiah Andrews, an English jeweler who set up shop in Philadelphia during the Revolutionary War. In his store he sold all kinds of jewelry, ladies' and gentlemen's shoe buckles, rings, lockets and brooches.

You might ask how it was that Robert, an amateur painter, obtained work in a jeweler's shop. The answer is found in the gold and silver lockets that were so much the fashion of that day and in the little chips of ivory that were inserted in the lockets and rings. With tiny brushes Fulton painted miniature portraits on the ivory, and soon became very skillful at this work. The money he earned went home to support his mother and sisters.

Robert's nineteenth birthday in 1784 found him a tall and uncommonly handsome young man, slight of build and dark-haired. His eyes, too, were dark and, being deep-set, seemed unusually expressive. He talked quietly yet with great persuasion and a sense of urgency. Even at this early age his appearance was one which commanded attention. And he showed another quality very often found in great men. That was his desire to learn and to work, for hours meant nothing to him.

It was work without rest, however—weeks, months and years of it—that soon broke down his health. The trouble seemed to be in his lungs. Doctors, worrying over his condition, urged him to move to a milder climate. So Robert packed

13

his paints and brushes and went to Bath, West Virginia, a "watering place" or kind of resort where people sought the curative power of natural springs bubbling from the ground.

Not only did his health improve at Bath, but also his fortunes. When the wealthy men there looked at the pictures he painted of them, they were most enthusiastic. "Mr. Fulton," one of them exclaimed, "you have talent! You should go to Europe to work under the finest artists. You ought to study with Benjamin West!" This was the same man, you recall, who grew up near near Robert's birthplace, and who had known his father. West had become so successful with his paintings and so famous, that he had gone to Europe where he had become the darling of the nobility—of counts, princes and even King George III.

Robert was glowing with better health when

he proudly returned to Philadelphia. We can easily imagine that painting miniatures and ivories for lockets seemed dull indeed compared with the prospect of painting the portraits of great men. But he did not have the money to go to Europe. Well, he would earn it! In 1786, when he was twenty, the following advertisement appeared in the newspaper:

ROBERT FULTON. Miniature painter and hair worker is removed from the northwest corner of Walnut and Second Streets to the West side of Front Street, one door above Pine Street, Philadelphia.

Here in his own shop he set to work with all his energy, for he had two goals—one to buy his mother and sisters a farm and then, after they were happily settled, to sail for Europe in the quest for fame and fortune.

By chance Robert's new shop was only a short block from the shores of the Delaware River

He earned money by painting miniatures

where, during these very months, an inventor
named John Fitch was riding up and down in
one of several steam-powered vessels he had designed. It is also a strange coincidence that William

Henry, the first man in America to attack the problem of building a steamboat, had been living in Lancaster where Robert grew up.

While the young painter was in Bath for his health, it also happened that in that very town the machinery was being built for still another trial steamboat designed by a man named James Rumsey. We will never know if Fulton ever saw any of these boats. Perhaps on his way home from his Philadelphia shop, he used to stop at the water front to watch the lazy sailboats and clumsy barges slowly making their way upriver. On these occasions he probably thought to himself: "Some day I shall invent a steamboat, and perhaps I may succeed where the others fail."

Perhaps his career as an artist filled his imagination at this time. In any event a great change in his life was awaiting him in the fall of 1786. During the year he had been in business for himself

Benjamin Franklin was interested in helping him

he had met a number of men like Benjamin
Franklin, who seemed interested in helping him.
Now that his family were contentedly settled on
their own farm, he needed only the money for
his passage to England. His friends in Philadelphia not only advanced this money, but also gave
him a letter to present to Benjamin West, the
painter, upon his arrival there.

18

It is not hard to imagine Robert's excitement when a fair breeze filled the sails of his ship as its bowsprit pointed east over the endless waters of the ocean. He was a poor farmer's son, but he was getting on in the world—and the whole world lay before him, a young man of twenty-one. As he stood on deck the wail of the wind whistling through the rigging filled his ears. Soon the last bit of land of his native country disappeared on the horizon to the west, and he and his hopes were alone.

3

HE TURNS INVENTOR

AFTER MANY LONG DAYS AT SEA ROBERT FULTON'S
excitement was boundless as the mist-shrouded
coast of England finally appeared in the distance.
His heart drummed like a tom-tom. Soon he
would be meeting the great man himself. He
would show Benjamin West the pictures he had
brought with him. He imagined Mr. West saying
to him: "Mr. Fulton, your work shows great skill
and imagination! Profit and even fame will come
to you here in England."

Presently he was hurrying through streets
gray with age and tradition. The sights and

sounds of a strange country filled his whole be-ing. At last he found himself at Benjamin West's door. The moment he had long dreamed of was at hand. As he entered the house, he was so tense that he was surprised he had any voice at all. "Mr. West, my name is Robert Fulton. Perhaps you remember my father. I have come from America. My home is in Lancaster." These were choppy sentences and not what he planned to say at all. Nervously he produced the letter of introduction to Mr. West.

With a smile Benjamin West put the young man at ease as he opened the letter. "I am glad to hear you are a painter, young man!"

"Yes sir," said Robert, his confidence coming back with a rush. "There are people in America who say that I have some talent. That is why I am here. I brought a couple of my pictures with

21

me." Eagerly he took his pictures out of a case. Mr. West studied them for a short time and then looked squarely at Robert.

"Mr. Fulton," he said. "Your friends are right. You do have talent. But the most that can be said for these pictures is that you show promise. Your talent is a youthful one. It may take years for you to develop into a really good painter."

The blood rushed to Robert's head. "There is all the difference in the world between a good picture and a great one," Benjamin West went on. "Work and more work—years of it—stand between you and your goal. I shall be glad to help, but you must not expect miracles overnight."

By the time Mr. West had finished visiting with him, Robert felt a little better. This had been a cruel disappointment. "Painting," he wrote his mother with all the pride he could summon, "requires more study than I at first imagined. I shall be obliged to stay here some time longer than I expected." We can sense the feeling of hopelessness, even fear, that struck him when he thought of the struggling days and months ahead. For he had arrived in England with very little money, and he had not the slightest idea of how he would earn his food and lodging when it was gone.

"I brought not more than 40 Guineas to England," he wrote home later, "and was set down in a strange country without a friend and only one letter of introduction to Mr. West. Here I had an art to learn by which I was to earn my bread, but little to support whilst I was doing it and numbers of Eminant men of the same profession which I must Excell before I Could hope to live. Many, Many a solitary hour I have spent

world. Then he would be able to save the money he earned.

But, finally, when he was about thirty years old he came to realize that painting would never bring him the rewards he sought, so he gave it up sorrowfully. His childhood dreams—that his pictures would one day capture the admiration of the whole world of art—had dissolved like mist. He found himself no farther along the rough trail toward fame and wealth than he had been ten years before.

Still full of ambition, however, he began to draw straighter arrows from his quiver. His new target was the wonderful world of invention. Had he forgotten his love for mechanical things— the gunshop he frequented as a boy, the paddle wheels he fastened to Peter Gumpf's fishing boat?

How was it during all these years as an artist that his inventive urge lay sleeping? There is no way of telling, but we do know that Robert now took up the draftsman's tools with the same confidence that had led him to take up the paintbrush. He invented a machine for sawing marble. For this he received a gold medal. He found a mechanical way to twist rope and received a patent on a machine that would spin flax. He wrote a book about canals and at the same time invented a number of devices having to do with this form of transportation.

From canals and canal boats his mind jumped nimbly to the problem of moving a boat by its own power and the possibility of designing a submarine. He was now at the threshold of an exciting period in his life—as exciting a life as that of any American pioneer thrusting his way into dark forests filled with unknown dangers. The tempting prospect of a steamboat was not quite so intriguing as building a vessel that would travel under the sea. If he could build such a craft, he would have a weapon that could threaten whole navies. By itself the submarine could, of course, destroy nothing. But he had in mind another invention which the submarine might carry—a torpedo.

Robert thought that if he could build a successful submarine, this invention might end all warfare, because no navy would be safe from the submarines of its enemy. Therefore countries would stop fighting. In this way he felt he would be serving the cause of peace in the world.

To the average person in 1797 the idea of torpedoes and submarines seemed as fantastic as space ships and flying saucers do to us. But a submarine that could travel great distances under water and torpedoes that would explode were about to be invented—and Robert Fulton was to be the inventor.

4

ENTER: THE SUBMARINE!

ABOARD THE SAILING VESSEL, TOSSING LIKE A
chip in the English Channel, were great numbers
of French people. Ever since they had come
aboard in England, they had been jabbering away
in their native tongue. Robert Fulton could not
understand a word of it. It had taken him years
to make his way in England. Now he was seeking his fortune in a new country, and perhaps it
was a mistake. These people were so different
from the English. His failure to understand them
brought back the painful feeling that he was very
much alone in the world.

Still, there was a great bond of sympathy between France and the United States because both countries were now republics. The spirit of liberty was in the air. As an American Fulton had far more in common with the republic of France than with the monarchy of England, from which America had so recently won its freedom. France and England were at swords' points. It seemed to Fulton that he would have little trouble interesting the French government in his plans for a submarine.

As he stood on deck, lost in thought, a Frenchman came up and started talking to him. Robert was bewildered. The more confused he became, the faster the Frenchman talked, walking up and down and waving his arms. At this moment a very pretty girl approached—a girl who did not seem like the others aboard the ship. In perfect English she told Robert what the Frenchman wanted. In French she then interpreted Robert's reply. The

Frenchman was satisfied, and Robert not only was grateful to the girl but wanted very much to know her better.

When the ship landed in Calais, he found himself once more trying to understand French officials who were asking him questions. And once more the girl smilingly came forward to help him. Through her he learned that there was something wrong with his papers. He would have to stay in Calais about three weeks before he could continue on to Paris. Although Robert had not known the girl the day before, she was beginning to crowd inventions out of his mind. He was determined to learn more about her, for he still did not even know her name.

At first she would not tell him, but at last she said that she was Madame François, the wife of a shopkeeper, and that she was returning home to join her husband. Robert's heart sank. But, as the days passed in Calais, he could not believe that she was married. She was beautiful and so young. There was something so aristocratic about her that she could not possibly be married to a lowly shopkeeper. Perhaps she was a member of the French nobility, who thus far had managed to escape the executioners.

Then he heard she was in trouble—that she had been locked up in a hotel room and was being guarded by French officials. Rushing to her room Robert cried breathlessly:

"Madame François, listen to me. You are in great danger and I can save you!"

"A thousand thanks," replied Madame François, "but be so kind as to explain."

"They are going to take you to Paris and put you in prison and once there, you are lost. Now listen to what I have to say. Nothing could be easier than to escape. Nothing could be more simple; marry me—do *marry me!*"

"Oh, thank you, but I am married already."

"Oh, what a shame, what a shame!" moaned Robert. "I could make you rich. I am going to make my fortune in Paris." Plans for building a submarine and torpedoes and many other inventions now tumbled from his lips. "It would be so easy to save you," he pleaded. "Only say the word and I will marry you, and that will be the end of your troubles."

Robert seemed to be very much in love, but he was to be disappointed once again. Although he did not learn it then, the girl really was one of the French nobility and unmarried. She was in temporary trouble from which she knew she would soon escape. The proposal which he made so suddenly and so earnestly she regarded very lightly. She certainly had no intention of rushing off into the unknown with Robert Fulton.

"I thanked him as seriously as I could," she wrote much later. "His little plan seemed to him *so simple*, and he proposed so kindly and heartily, that while I laughed, I could not help feeling grateful to him. I begged him not to trouble himself any more about me. . . . He sighed and departed."

Robert, crestfallen, had lost his chance to catch up with his sisters, who were now married and had children. He was an uncle to many, but as yet father to none. "However," he wrote home, "I am not old enough to grow musty, and possibly I may one day try how I like it. But at present there is not the most distant prospect."

As soon as his papers were in order, Robert journeyed on to Paris. There a wealthy American statesman named Joel Barlow took him in as a son. With Barlow and his wife, who had been living in France for some time, Fulton found the first home he had known in years. He started at once to try to interest French engineers in a system of canals which would link the tiniest French hamlets with the largest cities. While these ideas met with favor, nothing much was done about them. It was the submarine that caused excited whispers among the officials of France, and it was the submarine that now began to occupy all of Robert's thoughts.

Any swimmer knows that he can float if he holds his breath. If he exhales a little, he will start to sink, which means that he is now heavier than the water that has been holding him up. In the same way Fulton saw that it would be possible to build a watertight ship that would sink or float, depending upon how heavy it was. The main problem would be changing its weight while the crew were inside the ship. Robert solved this in the small model he was making by building in storage tanks. If the crew of the submarine wished to submerge, all they had to do was let water into the tanks. If they wanted to come up, they had merely to pump the water out of the tanks and turn a hand crank connected to a propeller on top of the vessel. This would lift it straight up, much like the rotor of a present-day helicopter.

To supply air to the crew, he planned to have a conning tower or pipe to thrust above the surface when the air inside needed changing. Another propeller turned by hand cranks from the inside would supply forward motion to the craft while submerged, and a sail would provide movement on the surface. At last, in 1798, Robert completed his model, which looked rather like a present-day blimp.

Could one say that he had *invented* the submarine at this point? Not really, because another American named David Bushnell had experimented earlier with an undersea craft. Although different from Fulton's in a number of ways, it had been much the same in others. An invention rarely springs full-fledged from the brain of one man. Rather, it seems to grow gradually, as an idea here and another idea there is grafted onto the original plan. And it is not an invention at all until someone shows that it will really work. That was Robert Fulton's goal.

Thus far he had only a model, which he now tried to show the French government. This was harder than he had supposed. The Revolution against the French monarchy had left the country strained and uneasy. Napoleon was about to seize the reins of power. Robert still thought of his submarine as an instrument of peace; and in a letter to Napoleon he said that the strong navies of the world, particularly that of England, were preventing free trade among nations. He felt that the submarine would end this monopoly of the seas. No navy would be safe from an undersea vessel stealthily gliding under water at night into the very midst of the enemy fleet.

At last the French government appointed some experts to examine Fulton's model. While there were some things they thought should be changed, the experts were enthusiastic, declaring that Robert was "a man of genius." They described his weapon as "a terrible method of destruction, since it acts in silence." But they did not think that the time had yet come for the government to try to build these vessels and start out across the English Channel to attack the British Navy.

Fulton, they declared, would first have to build a full-sized submarine. Then he would have to select one or two companions as a crew and practice running the ship under water. And he would still have to find a good method of attaching his "torpedoes" to the hulls of enemy ships. All this would take time, the experts said. However, in their view the government surely ought to give Fulton money to build a full-sized submarine.

But the French government still made no move to assist Robert with funds to build his ship. "One has an idea," he thought bitterly. "He spends weeks and months making the drawings. He at last completes a model which is approved by famous men chosen by the government to examine it. Then the government turns its back on the invention!" Did such obstacles strew the path of every inventor? Would he *ever* reach the position in the world that he had first sought as an artist, and now sought as a man devoted to the mechanical arts?

No one ever accomplished anything by bemoaning his luck. The only thing to do was to fight inaction with action. Somehow—somehow he would raise the money to build the submarine himself, and he now started out to accomplish this. If you did not know, you would never guess the means Robert chose to do it. He bought an English patent for what was called a "panorama." Forming a company, he built a kind of theater not far from the Boulevard Montmartre. On the inside walls he painted gigantic murals of a great fire that had not long before ravaged the city of Moscow in Russia. So dramatic, so vivid were the flames he painted roaring through the streets of that city, with tongues of fire leaping from a thousand windows, that all Paris came and paid to see his exhibit. In this way he raised the money to build his submarine.

About this time Robert was walking along the

*Robert met Madame François again on a street in
Paris*

street in Paris one day when suddenly he looked up and saw a lovely, familiar face. It was Madame François, the girl who had helped him with his papers when he first arrived in France! Running up to her and her escort, Robert seized her by both hands.

"Madame François, how glad I am to see you!" As we know, her name was not Madame François at all. But it was indeed the same girl, and Fulton had happened to meet her while she was strolling with her brother-in-law. The brother-in-law, knowing nothing of her previous experience with Fulton, said:

"Monsieur, the person to whom you have the honor of speaking is Mademoiselle de Montaut."

"No, no!" Robert protested. "It is Madame François. She is married; she told me in Calais. But what did you say? Mademoiselle what? Mademoiselle de Montaut?" Taking out a slip of paper, he wrote down "Mademoiselle de Montaut" and stuffed it back in his pocket. Then he began to tell of his inventions. "Monsieur, I have come to Paris on a wonderful mission—to blow up vessels, to run boats under the rivers and to run them on the surface by steam power."

"My brother," recalled Mademoiselle de Montaut much later, "thought he was absolutely mad; and, cutting short the conversation, we did not see him again."

5

A DARING VOYAGE

EVEN TODAY WHEN YOU BUILD SOMETHING THAT has never been built before, much of it must be done by hand. But at least you have good steel to work with and all kinds of machinery to help shape the various pieces. In forging the parts for his submarine, Robert had to depend almost entirely on blacksmiths. Blacksmiths are rare today, but if you have ever seen one, you know what a tedious job it is to shape an object with quick blows of a heavy hammer, then return the object to the forge to heat it red-hot again so that further shaping can be done.

Think of the weeks and months it took to

build Robert's submarine—of the problems to be conquered, of the mistakes to be corrected. Compared with today's submarines his was a toy, with its hand cranks and propellers. But it was the forerunner of the powerful undersea ship of today, just as the Wright Brothers' flimsy flying machine was the great-grandfather of all aircraft.

From dawn until dark Robert haunted Périer's workshop in Rouen where his ship was being built. Gradually it took shape until, one day in 1800, its proud young builder could say that it was finished. The French government had given him no help but was glad to have an official committee on hand for the trial trip.

News reached many ears that the *Nautilus*—as Robert called his submarine—would be tested in July. Early in the morning of the day that the test took place a crowd had already gathered on the banks of the river Seine. The *Nautilus* was floating in the river, and Robert with two sailors was getting ready to submerge. At length the official inspection committee arrived with Mr. Forfait, the Minister of the Marine in Napoleon's cabinet.

"We shall now enter the *Nautilus*," Robert announced just before the trial trip, "dive to the bottom of the river, and remain submerged for forty-five minutes. This experiment will prove that in this ship it is possible to live for a long period under the sea. Here the shallowness of the river will not permit us to move about under water. However, we hope the value of an invisible ship that is at home under the waves will become clear to the most doubtful observer."

Scarcely a whisper could be heard in the crowd on the bank as the two sailors climbed down into the *Nautilus*, followed by Robert, who shut the escape hatch after him. Proceeding slowly along the surface to deeper water, the strange craft stopped. Then, after a few moments, it began to sink. Soon nothing was visible except the bulge in the top where the hatch was located. Seconds later that, too, disappeared. The observers on the bank, craning their necks, could hardly believe what they were seeing.

"It is a foolish experiment," one of them said.

"They are trapped like rats!" muttered another.

As the minutes ticked by and there was not the slightest sign of motion near the spot where the *Nautilus* had gone down, hope for the occupants of the strange craft began to fade away. When forty-five endless minutes had passed and there was still no sign of the submarine, the official inspectors looked at one another gravely, shrugged their shoulders and whispered in low tones. The crowd was silent.

Presently, near the spot where the *Nautilus*

47

had gone down, bubbles could be seen. In a few seconds a gray form appeared. A shout went up from the bank. Within minutes the *Nautilus* was in full view again. Suddenly the door on the top opened; and the tall, lithe figure of Robert Fulton appeared! Cheers now rang out from the bank. The government inspectors were talking excitedly among themselves. One had to see such an exhibition to believe it. Unquestionably the submarine would become a great weapon of the sea.

All eyes were fastened on the inventor and the two members of his crew as they approached the bank. Robert's face, lighted with smiles, was a study in modesty mixed with pride.

"Monsieur," announced the Minister of the Marine, Mr. Forfait, "I have no doubt of the value of your machine. This has been a great spectacle!"

Robert went home that night as tired and as

Cheers arose as Robert emerged from the
NAUTILUS

happy as the victor in an athletic contest. The
Minister of the Marine had promised to send
Napoleon a most enthusiastic report of the
Nautilus. Through Mr. Forfait it seemed certain
that a loan of 6,000 francs would be obtained
from the French government to pay for further

experiments. Although this was but a fraction of the 28,000 francs of his own money that Robert had had to spend, it was better than nothing. And probably more money would be coming from the government later.

But his hopes were to be dashed again. Weeks passed and the government did nothing. All Robert was able to get from Napoleon was a statement in writing that if he were captured by the British during his experiments at sea, he would be treated like any French sailor who had fallen into the hands of the enemy. If the British did not treat him in such a manner, then the French government would take revenge upon British captives held in France.

Spending his own money, Robert now decided to try out his submarine in the English Channel. The craft was towed down the river Seine to the seaport of Le Havre, where the inventor was able to practice in deep water off the shore. Making repeated dives, Fulton and his two sailors tested the hand cranks connected to the propellers and perfected the torpedoes. It was at this point that he decided upon a three-man attack against the British Navy, which today seems absurd. Through the French Intelligence, he planned to find out where the English ships were anchored. Then he and his crew would set out one day across the English Channel to reach them, traveling much of the way on the surface.

Outside the harbor where the English ships were anchored, the submarine would dive and steal shoreward until it was beside a British man-of-war. There Fulton would affix his torpedo to the hull of the enemy ship, turn about and make all possible headway toward the open sea. As he withdrew, an explosion would rock the water, and there would be one less British frigate strangling the freedom of the seas. To our ears this scheme sounds as foolhardy as sailing over an enemy anti-aircraft battery in a gas balloon, but Robert none the less embarked upon it.

On September 12, 1800, he and his crew of two sailors set out from France into the English Channel. Rocking along the surface with the aid of a sail affixed to the top of the submarine, the three adventurers at first met good weather. Their destination, a point a little over seven miles from the Marcou Islands, might have been reached in fairly good time except for a series of storms. Wild enough on fair days, the Channel writhed with jagged waves, battering the *Nautilus* about like a barrel. When the skies cleared and the submarine proved to be still watertight, it proceeded on its course. At last it reached its destination, a small harbor where British ships were known to ride at anchor.

The sailors turned the crank as Robert steered

Robert chose midnight as the hour for his attack. In a calm sea he furled his sail, descende'd into the dank interior of the ship, closed the hatch after him and opened a valve. A rush of water filled the ballast tanks, and the *Nautilus* began to

sink. Down the three men went, crowded together in the tiny chamber, a flickering candle
casting strange shadows on its sweating iron
walls. At once the sailors began to turn the hand
cranks as Robert guided their course with his
compass and barometer. The *Nautilus* labored
forward.

"Faster, boys!" urged Robert, breaking a long
silence. "We will never make it if the tide turns
before we reach the harbor!" The sailors re-
doubled their efforts, their legs cramped and ach-
ing, their arms taut and strained as they tugged
at the clumsy cranks. For a few minutes the
Nautilus moved briskly forward, but then she began to slow down despite the mighty efforts of
the two sailors at their cranks. Now the ship was
almost at a standstill.

"We are too late," said Fulton in despair. "The
tide has turned!" Breathing heavily the crewmen

relaxed at their cranks. Robert pumped water out of the ballast tanks and turned the propeller on top of the vessel. The *Nautilus* began to rise until she was just below the surface. The pipes to admit air to the compartment were thrust up, and the candle was blown out to conserve oxygen. Finally the anchor was dropped.

"We are so close to our target," announced Fulton, "that they would spot us if we were to surface. We must remain submerged until the next tide."

Silence now filled the damp compartment, only four feet high, as the men stretched their legs as best they could and prepared to sit out the opposing tide, which would run for six hours. Little was said. With nothing to do, the two sailors' imaginations ran to thoughts of death by drowning or possibly by explosion. Suppose the British should see their air pipe at dawn! Never should they have embarked on this crazy voyage! Now it was too late, and their only choice was to see it through.

As for Robert, he was thinking only of the task ahead. No possibility other than success even suggested itself. Daylight would come with the next tide; but if they remained submerged, there would be little chance of being discovered.

The six endless hours passed. When the *Nautilus* swung about on its anchor chain, Robert realized that the tide had turned. Hurriedly the ventilators were drawn down, the anchor hauled in and ballast tanks filled. As the vessel began to sink, the sailors returned to their cranks and Robert to his instruments. At length the *Nautilus* found its way into the harbor toward its objective. The torpedoes were placed in readiness. The crucial moment had come!

But had it? In the next few moments Fulton

realized his bitter bad luck. In the interval between the tides the two British ships had hoisted
sail and departed. At first he could not bring himself to believe this, but when the *Nautilus* cautiously surfaced and he could view the full sweep
of the harbor, there was no doubt that they were
gone. "Fulton luck!" he moaned as he climbed
wearily back into the compartment. Now the
Nautilus turned about for the long journey back
to France, which it reached without further
trouble.

That fall he sailed on another expedition
against the same two ships, but they eluded him
once more. He found that the watchful British
Intelligence had learned of his plans and had
warned the commanders of the brigs. Now it was
turning cold, and he had to put the *Nautilus* up
for the winter. In the meantime he never relaxed
his campaign to interest the French government,

which finally granted him 10,000 francs for further experiments. A liberal prize in money was added for any ship he managed to sink. This was encouraging as Robert had already spent more than three times this amount from his own money.

During the following year he worked hard on new ideas for a larger submarine that would stay under water for eight hours, and on better methods of releasing his torpedoes. All this effort was costing him more money. Meanwhile the French government was still sitting on the fence waiting to see how he came out before granting him any large sum. Faced with such apathy, he could not continue forever as a combination inventor, financier and undersea navy. Even if it was not his nature to give up, he still had to yield to such odds. Perhaps he was a "visionary." Perhaps his submarine was, after all, just a "mad scheme."

Some men succeed very young in this world. Others are old by the time they achieve their aims. And of course a great many, perhaps the majority, never really succeed at all. In 1801 Robert had reached the age of thirty-six. He was not old, but his youth was certainly behind him. He had failed as an artist, and he had not truly succeeded as an inventor. But defeat sometimes serves merely to spur the defeated on to greater efforts.

So it was with Robert Fulton, who had rare spirit. Each defeat had left him abler and stronger. Now he had come to the threshold of his greatest adventure.

6

HIS FIRST STEAMBOAT

ROBERT WAS STILL DEEP IN THE BATTLE TO prove the value of his submarine when a wealthy American, Chancellor Robert R. Livingston, arrived in Paris. A Hudson River landholder and a power in the state of New York, Livingston had sworn in George Washington as the first President of the United States. Now at the peak of his career as a statesman, the Chancellor was taking up his post as American Ambassador to France.

Livingston also thought of himself as an inventor, although he was very much an amateur in mechanics. For our story it is important only that he was interested in steam power. As we have seen, what inventors like Robert needed was the help of men who had money which they were willing to spend on experiments. Livingston had long been interested in the possibility of steamships. Upon his arrival in Paris in November, 1801, he had heard a great deal about a clever young American inventor named Robert Fulton, and it was not long before the two men met.

We can imagine that Robert immediately started talking about submarines and continued to do so until Chancellor Livingston, an impatient man, cut him off. "Mr. Fulton, I am not interested in submarines. I am interested in harnessing the power of steam to boats. Have you ever thought about that?"

"Yes, sir, I have indeed!" we can hear Robert saying with his usual eagerness. "In England a number of years ago I designed a boat whose method of propulsion was like that of a fish. My idea was to have a steam engine move a stern paddle back and forth like a fish's tail, thus driving the boat forward."

"How did that work out?" asked Livingston skeptically.

"There were many problems in perfecting that design so I hit upon another. I built a model and attached paddle wheels to the bow. The model boat was long, narrow, and had a flat bottom so that it would not take up so much space in the water. I wrote the English makers, Boulton and Watt, asking them if they could make me an engine of three or four horsepower which could be placed in a boat. But they were not interested. I put the boat aside as I was then busy with other projects."

"I understand," said Livingston. "But how did the paddle wheels work out on your model?"

"I am sure that the best method of propelling a steamship is with paddle wheels," said Robert. "I found that a wheel with three or six paddles was best. With any other number the paddles seemed to work against each other."

"Many men have tried to invent a successful steamship," said Chancellor Livingston at length. "Some of them have actually built boats that would run. But for one reason or another all of them have failed. The world is waiting for a ship that will sail without depending upon winds or tides. The man who invents it will become rich. I will also predict that he will become famous. Mr. Fulton, I believe that you can design a successful steamship. Do you want to try?"

"I know it can be done, sir," said Robert. "It just requires patience. One must find out why the others have failed so as to avoid their mistakes. Certainly it can be done. Yes, sir, I should like to try."

"Good for you!" said the Chancellor warmly. He shook Robert's hand. "I shall stand behind you and help in every way I can."

In October, 1802, Robert Fulton and Chancellor Livingston signed an agreement. It provided that Livingston would advance the money for a trial steamboat to be designed and built by Robert. If this was a success, Robert was to build another boat in America to run between New York and Albany on the Hudson River.

As eagerly as a hound tracking a rabbit, Robert searched for the magic formula for assembling paddle wheels, gears, engine and boiler in a combination that would successfully propel a boat. Why had steamboats built by earlier inventors failed? If these men had good ideas, why were they good? If they had made mistakes, what were the reasons? "All these things being governed by the laws of nature," wrote Robert, "the real invention is to find them. Till the artist knows the necessary proportions, he must work in the dark and cannot be said to have made any clear and distinct discovery or useful invention."

Before starting to build his boat, Robert attached paddles of various kinds to a small model whose power came from two clock springs. By watching the four-foot model perform on a pond he was able to avoid many costly errors. He determined once and for all that paddle wheels were the best means of driving a boat. Then he proceeded to solve his other main problem which was how to transmit all possible power from the engine to the paddle wheels.

At last he decided that the time had come to build the boat. It was to be 70 feet long, 8 feet wide and 3 feet high. The paddle wheels were to be 12 feet in diameter. For the actual building of the boat he chose the Périer Brothers' shop on the bank of the Seine where his submarine had been constructed. Now came slow days of hand labor—of sawing and fitting planks for the hull of the boat, of hammering out each part large and small for the mechanism which was to carry power from the steam engine to the paddle wheels.

He did not think it necessary to build his own engine as a number of earlier inventors had done. Rather he chose to rent one of eight horsepower from the Périer shop. The steam engine had been invented very recently and was then used mainly to pump water out of English coal mines. There were a few of these engines in France, and it was one of these that Robert decided to place in his boat. Of course this engine was not built for a

66

boat, but Robert thought he could make it over so that it would perform satisfactorily.

Exciting days passed one by one. Finally, in the spring of 1803, Robert Fulton's first steamboat lay completed below Périer's shop on the bank of the Seine. Late one night, shortly before the day chosen for the trial run, he awoke to the rumbling of a furious storm outside and a loud pounding on his door.

"Mr. Fulton! Mr. Fulton!" cried a voice out of the night. "The boat has broken to pieces and gone to the bottom!" Not even taking time to put on a coat, Robert dashed out into the storm and sprinted to the river bank. There a pitiful sight met his eyes. Where his boat had been tied up that afternoon, there were now only waves flecked with driving rain. For a few minutes he stood looking dazedly at the spot, gripped by an

67

*Robert was gripped by an overpowering sense of
defeat*

overpowering sense of defeat. Then, numbly, he began to think what could be done to raise the boat.

He never returned home that night, nor the next day, nor the following evening; nor did he even stop to eat. Drenched to the skin he labored mightily for twenty-four hours, and at last he managed to raise his boat. Only then did he stagger back home. Finding him ill from long exposure and overexertion, the doctor ordered him to remain in bed. But Robert would not stay there. Feeling that he was desperately needed, he was soon back at the water front supervising repairs, all the while feeling so sick that he could hardly stand.

Why had the boat sunk? Apparently he had made a serious mistake in its design. The boiler and engine were so heavy that the framework had not been strong enough to hold them, especially in a storm. Now, wearily, he set about correcting this defect.

As the days passed, his strength gradually returned and so did his cheerful optimism. The repairs went well and he named August 9, 1803, as the date for the trial trip. Meanwhile the Emperor Napoleon, who had more or less ignored the submarine, was paying closer attention to the steamboat. He had changed his opinion of Robert, whom he had formerly considered a dreamer. Complaining that his navy minister should have told him sooner about Fulton's steamboat, Napoleon claimed that "It may change the face of the world."

The Emperor realized that if the steamship had been perfected earlier a full-scale invasion of England might have been possible. A large number of ships could have been built to tow barges filled with French soldiers across the Channel to

England. If the day chosen had been one with no wind, the British sailing ships would have been powerless to stop the barge and steamboat fleet. However fanciful this may seem, it at least proved one thing—Robert's efforts as an inventor were for the first time being taken seriously by the public at large.

The day of the trial, August 9th, arrived. Robert was in high spirits as he started a wood fire in his boiler, which presently began to sing with steam. During the day he adjusted the machinery carefully and counseled the three men who were to serve as his crew. As the afternoon progressed, people began to gather on the river bank. Shortly before six o'clock, the hour of the trial, various officials of the French Navy and government appeared. A few minutes before six Robert made a final check of the engine. All seemed to be in order. A fine hot fire glowed under the boiler, which had a good pressure of steam. A column of smoke poured from the smokestack, to the amazement of the bystanders.

At six o'clock Robert turned a valve. A rush of steam filled the cylinder of the engine. With a groan the piston started to move. The huge side wheels began to turn, one paddle after another striking the water. The steamboat began to move. Gathering momentum, it soon reached the speed

The steamboat ran back and forth along the Seine

of a fast walk, and a cheer went up from the spectators on the bank.

For an hour and a half Robert ran his steamboat back and forth along the Seine. He turned, stopped and started a dozen times to show that he could control his craft at will. He even towed two other vessels to prove the power of his boat.

When the trial was over, the government officials pressed forward from the crowd and overwhelmed Robert with compliments. At last he had become the man of the hour, even to thousands who had not witnessed the trial run. A French newspaper described it as "a boat . . . with two large wheels mounted on an axle like that of a chariot, while behind these wheels was a kind of large stove with a pipe, as if there were some kind of a small fire engine intended to operate the wheels." For an hour and a half Robert

Fulton "produced the curious spectacle of a boat moved by wheels, like a chariot."

The steamboat was a success—that is, it was a success as far as the public was concerned. But secretly Robert was disturbed. Actually the trial was a disappointment to him. He had been sure that his boat would go ten miles an hour, and it had only gone three or four. That was not fast enough. He would have to start all over again.

7

OTHERS WHO TRIED

A TEAKETTLE IS THE BEST EVERYDAY EXAMPLE of the power of steam. When someone forgets to turn off the burner, and the water in the kettle is boiling, you have probably watched the cover jump up and down as steam pours out of the spout. If the spout is closed for a moment, the boiling water continues to turn into steam which now has no place to go. It starts putting pressure on the inside of the kettle. It pushes harder and harder against the cover which soon hops up and down in a merry jig as the steam escapes from under it.

The principle of a steam engine is based simply

on the fact that water boils and turns into steam at 212 degrees Fahrenheit. If the steam is not allowed to escape, but is shut up in a vessel or boiler, it builds up tremendous pressure. If the steam is released a little at a time from the boiler, it will push whatever is in its way. In an engine the escaping steam pushes a piston. Moving back and forth inside a cylinder, the piston is connected with a crank which turns the wheels. That is

76

about all there is to the simplest kind of steam engine.

Yet how long it took mankind not only to discover what steam would do, but to harness it to an engine! The problems Robert Fulton faced in trying to build a successful steamboat can be appreciated only when you know that it took centuries for the steam engine to develop and then to find its way into ships.

Two hundred years before Christ, a Greek named Hero the Younger showed what steam could do and used it to open and close the doors of a temple. From that time *two thousand* years passed before inventors developed a steam engine that was really any good. During the 1100's, steam was used to play a European organ. Three hundred years later men began to think about steam engines and even to draw plans, but they did nothing further.

One hundred and thirty-eight years after Columbus discovered America, an Englishman named the Marquis of Worcester actually built a steam engine. Then came other Englishmen— Thomas Savery, Thomas Newcomen, and at last, James Watt, each one improving on the engines of the others. By the time Robert Fulton built his first steamboat in France, the steam engine was strong enough to turn paddle wheels.

The invention of the steam engine was one thing and sending it to sea in a boat was quite another. In 1707 a Frenchman named Denis Papin tried it, but some ignorant boatmen, thinking Papin's boat was created by witchcraft, destroyed it, and the inventor fled from the country. Later an English clockmaker named Jonathan Hulls designed and tried to build a steamboat but was laughed out of town while his neighbors sang:

Jonathan Hulls
With his patent skulls
Invented a machine
To go against wind and stream;
But he, being an ass,
Couldn't bring it to pass,
And so was ashamed to be seen.

A few years before the Revolutionary War a Frenchman, Count Joseph d'Auxiron, designed and built a steamboat, but that too was sunk by neighboring boatmen who were hostile to anything that was not a sailboat.

After this unhappy man came a young French nobleman named the Marquis de Jouffroy, who built a steamer 130 feet long with paddle wheels, which he demonstrated in 1783. This boat ran for fifteen minutes and then collapsed. Nevertheless, he was probably the first man in history to run a boat under its own power. The French government would not grant him a patent unless he gave

79

another demonstration in Paris. Discouraged, Jouffroy gave up.

Then there was William Symington of England who built a steamer called the *Charlotte Dundas* in 1801. This boat ran from five to seven miles an hour and was used for towing barges on the canals. Then the man died who had been supplying Symington with money, and he too gave up further experiments.

Meanwhile, what had been happening in America? You will remember that William Henry, who came from Robert Fulton's home town of Lancaster, was designing steamboats as early as 1770 when Robert was only six years old. During the 1780's, James Rumsey built three different steamboats, two in America and one in England. Poor Rumsey died just when he seemed to be on the verge of success.

A ragged, gangling farmer's son named John

Robert simply would not give up

Fitch came closer to success than any of these other men. At first he built several boats that were all failures, but finally he managed to construct not only a boat but an engine that ran several thousand miles on the Delaware River during the summer of 1790. He failed because the people were afraid of his boat and would not ride. John Fitch died a disappointed and poverty-sticken man.

A Vermont and New Hampshire genius named Samuel Morey was known to have traveled the Connecticut River in a tiny side-wheel steamboat as early as 1790. There were still others, such as Elijah Ormsbee of Rhode Island, John Stevens and William Longstreet of New Jersey, and Oliver Evans of Delaware. All of them tried and, for one reason or another, all failed.

Nor had Robert Fulton as yet succeeded. His first steamboat was just a curiosity. Other inventors before him had managed to get more speed out of their boats. Now, in the fall of 1803, the world still awaited the building of a steamboat sturdy enough and fast enough to challenge several thousand years of travel by sailing ship.

Was Robert the man to build it? Perhaps he was. Perhaps one quality alone made him more of a man than all these others who had gone before him—he had tremendous courage. He had suffered as many defeats and disappointments as any of them. But he simply would not give up.

8

SECRETS OF
A PRISONER

ROBERT COULD NEVER FORGET HIS SUBMARINE.
Even when his thoughts were taken up with his
first steamboat, he was wishing that he could
build still another undersea craft. Joel Barlow, in
whose Paris home Robert lived for seven years,
tried to persuade "Toot," as he called Robert, to
do one thing at a time.

"Toot is calling for funds," Barlow wrote a
friend. "Besides the 3,000 (francs) which I must
pay him tomorrow, and 3,000 more at the end
of the month, he wants 3,000 more still to build
a new boat (submarine) at Brest. I see no end

A mysterious visitor talked with Robert behind closed doors

to it; he is plunging deeper all the time, and if he doesn't succeed, I don't know what will become of him." Barlow managed to hold the younger man down, at least while he was building his steamboat.

But then, shortly after Robert made his successful trial run, a mysterious visitor named Mr. Smith arrived in Paris to talk with him behind closed doors.

"Mr. Fulton," said Smith with an air of secrecy, "the British want to use your submarine against the French fleet." This was an astonishing announcement. It took a few minutes for Robert to arrange his thoughts.

"I don't know why they want it," he said at last. "Some day my submarine will also destroy the British Navy. That is what it will certainly do."

"That may well be," said Smith, "but the

British want it just the same." Robert's face was furrowed in deep thought. While he had lived in England for a number of years and had many friends there, he was no admirer of the British Empire. Even less did he like its strong navy sweeping the seas. Although Napoleon had ignored his submarine, was that reason enough to consider doing business with an enemy of France? Probably not.

Yet a great invention, like a masterpiece of art, was not really the property of one country. It belonged to the world. Perhaps the best way to bring the submarine into general use was to let the British have it. Before long the fleets of the world would have to stop fighting or be sunk by each other's submarines.

This reasoning may sound strange to us. It may sound disloyal. But we must remember that because he was an American Robert could not feel any real loyalty to England or France. He simply did not care which of two foreign countries adopted his submarine. He passionately believed that the sooner somebody adopted it the sooner warfare would come to an end on the seas. Of one thing he was certain. No longer would the officials of a rich nation stand around ignoring him while he spent every cent of his own money on an invention of interest to them.

"Mr. Smith," he said at last. "I am busy here in France with the steamboat. If I go to England to build a submarine and prove its value, I must have 10,000 pounds. When it is completed and proven, I will sell the invention to the government for 100,000 pounds. That is the cost of only one British ship of the line. And I must have an agreement in writing."

"To bring such an agreement in writing to

France at this time," replied Smith, "would be very dangerous."

"So it would," reflected Robert. "All right. I will go to Holland and you can bring the answer in writing to me there." This was satisfactory to Smith and he departed. When the time for their second meeting approached, Robert went to Holland. A week—two—three—a month went by, without a word from Smith. For three months Robert waited in vain and then returned in disgust to France.

Finally one day, a quiet knock sounded on the door. It was Smith again with a reply from the British written in secret code. The message said that the British could not agree to Robert's demand for money, but if he would only go to England he could be sure of getting the best kind of treatment from the government.

89

With a heavy heart Robert left Paris for England in the spring of 1804. He had no clear idea that he would get anything at all for his submarine from the British. If the past treatment he had received from the French government was any proof, his visit to London would probably amount to nothing. But he felt that he had to go. He knew that if he did not, he would lose not only the submarine, but the steamboat.

You will remember that when he built his steamboat he had an agreement with Chancellor Livingston. It provided that Robert would build another boat for the Hudson River in America if his first one in Paris succeeded. It had succeeded although Robert had been disappointed in its speed. In order to build the American steamboat, Robert needed a steam engine from the expert English makers, Boulton and Watt. He had already placed an order for this engine, but Boulton and Watt had written him that the British government would not let them send the engine to America. The reason for this was that English officials were now going to deal with Robert on the submarine. They knew that they could force him to do as they wished, for if he didn't they would not let him have the engine for his steamboat. Robert, the victim of a kind of blackmail, was thus quite helpless. The outcome of both the steamboat and the submarine would depend upon the whims of Englishmen in high places.

After his arrival he tried to get the government officials to act promptly concerning the submarine. He was told to wait, and this he did for five weeks. Finally he became so upset that he could not sleep. He wrote the government that during these long weeks he had been treated almost like a prisoner. He had come to England in good faith, believing that the government would keep its promises. Was it going to keep them or not? He wanted to know right away.

At last he was told that a government committee had looked over his plans for a submarine, but that they were not interested in it. Actually the British had invited Fulton to Britain to keep him from perfecting the submarine for use by the French. His torpedo might prove useful by itself, and the government might want to build some of those. But Robert would have to wait for his money until they tested the torpedo. Robert was furious. But he knew that showing his temper would accomplish nothing. What chance had an American farmer's son against the British Empire? Far better to be patient and accept what money they were willing to pay him. Otherwise they would never give Boulton and Watt permission to send the engine for his steamboat to America.

The government at last agreed to pay Robert 7,000 pounds for expenses and 200 pounds a month salary while he was in England. Since the Prime Minister was interested in the torpedo, Robert was to make some of them and try them out against the French Navy.

It was with a very heavy heart that Robert went to Portsmouth to build torpedoes. He was nervous and despondent. He felt so ill that he could eat next to nothing. Night after night he would lie awake in his lonely room thinking of his unhappiness. There was no chance now for his submarine. As for the torpedo—that would merely make the English Navy stronger, and he did not want to do that. He had always thought of the submarine as a liberator of the seas. Now that idea had to be given up, and he was being used by the government as a kind of ammunition factory to build torpedoes. These were to be carried at night by surface rafts and tied to the anchor chains of French ships which Napoleon was preparing for an invasion against England. Robert did not want any part of that. "But if I do not remain here," he thought, "they will never give me permission to take my steamboat engine to America!"

On October 21, 1805, England won its famous victory over the French at Trafalgar. The British Navy ruled the seas once more, and the government began to lose all interest in Robert's torpedoes. The inventor received little more than enough to pay his expenses during his two years in England. But the government did give Boulton and Watt permission to send his steamboat engine to America.

Robert's experience in England had been a nightmare, and he was anxious to forget it.

9

HOMEWARD BOUND

In the fall of 1806 Robert left for America on a fine sailing packet. How much had happened since that faraway day twenty years before, when from a similar ship he had strained his eyes for a first look at the shores of England! He remembered how he had hurried through the streets of London, eager to present to Benjamin West a letter that would start him on his career as an artist.

How long it took a person to accomplish great things! What powerful forces had arrayed themselves against him! The world of invention was no place for a faint-hearted man. And how much one had to sacrifice! Here he was forty-two years old and he had not yet found a wife, to say nothing of the means to support her.

Robert smiled as he thought of the beautiful girl whom he had seen some weeks before in London sitting in a box at the opera. He had recognized her as his mysterious friend, Mademoiselle de Montaut!

She was sitting in the Duke of Portland's box beside Lord Clarendon. He could not believe his eyes—the last he'd met her was in Paris. When she saw Robert looking up at her, she smiled and bowed. At this Robert rushed up to seize her hands.

"What a pleasure, Mlle. de Montaut, to find you again here! I could hardly believe it was you."

"Monsieur," said one of the lady's French companions, "you are in error, for Madame is

96

the Viscountess of Gontaut." The others in the box laughed.

"This is too much," exclaimed Robert, "always changing your name! It is enough to drive one mad. But I see that these gentlemen are in on the mystery. If it is a joke, let us laugh together."

"The joke," said the Viscountess of Gontaut, "has been carried far enough. Mr. Fulton, now that we are in England I am happy to explain everything. I am the daughter of Count Montaut Navailles. My father was in the Court of Louis XVI. On the eve of the Revolution, we were able to escape to England, otherwise we would have been executed with the others. But someone had to return to France to look after family matters, so I made the journey under an assumed name. . . ."

"Madame François!" volunteered Robert.

"Yes," laughed the Viscountess, "Madame François. It was on that journey that I helped you with your passport. For me it was a dangerous trip. When we met the second time in Paris, it was still not possible to tell you who I was. Since then I have really married and am now the wife of Viscount Gontaut-Biron."

"I see," said Robert. "Well, I am glad that this mystery is solved at last." After meeting the others in the box Robert returned to his seat. It was the last time he ever saw her.

Meanwhile he met a rich English widow whom he thought seriously of asking to be his wife. When he wrote of his plan to Mr. and Mrs. Barlow, who had recently moved from Paris to America, he received an immediate reply. Begging him not to marry the English widow, Barlow pointed out that her education and feelings were English. "And what is perhaps more unfortunate

98

for you, she has a fortune." Barlow said that the English woman could never be happy in America and Robert would never be happy in England. "As to her fortune," the older man added, "I would rather take you with what you now have than with all the money in the world."

So Robert did not marry the English widow. Instead he began to make plans for his return to America. Since it was possible that something might happen to his ship on the return voyage, he wrote Barlow that he was leaving complete sets of drawings of his submarine and steamboat in England. He put them in a tin cylinder with his will and left them with a friend named General Lyman. He requested Barlow to publish all his inventions if anything should happen to him on the voyage home. Robert wanted the world to know about the steamboat and how the submarine would bring freedom to the seas.

*Robert arrived in America in high spirits and good
health*

The voyage home was safe and uneventful. As Robert's ship neared the shores of America, a deep feeling for his country welled up within him. After twenty years he was returning to his own people—to the familiar scenes and sounds of his homeland. This was an overpowering experience. As he disembarked from the ship in December, 1806, even the air seemed different. He was in high spirits and in better health than he had known for a long time. He had the financial backing of Chancellor Livingston. Now he felt equal to the biggest task of his life—the task of building the *North River Steamboat of Clermont*.

10

THE GREAT JOURNEY OF THE CLERMONT

AS SOON AS HE LANDED, ROBERT WENT TO Washington where his good friend, Mr. Barlow, was living. In detail he told the older man of his experiences since he had left Paris. He discussed his plans for the new boat on the Hudson River. As always, Barlow was an eager listener and a wise counselor. While enjoying a vacation in the house of the man who had really become his foster father, Robert took pleasure in designing a summerhouse for the lawn of Barlow's estate.

In a few months he returned to New York to supervise the building of his new steamboat at the shipyard of Charles Brownne at Corlear's Hook on the East River in New York. His precious steam engine from the shop of Boulton and Watt had crossed the Atlantic in crates, and he took as much pleasure in unpacking them as if he were opening Christmas presents.

The spring of 1807 had arrived, and spring was the time for ship building. The salt air blowing in from the sea had lost its sting. The strong sun warmed the fingers of the carpenters as they joined the timbers of the hull. Robert was busy with a hundred details. He was so interested in the progress of the boat that he could not leave, and besides, the workmen were always asking questions. In the building of a sailing ship they needed no advice—but who in America had had any experience in building a boat which had to be strong enough to hold several tons of machinery?

Robert supervised the building of his new steamboat

At length the vessel was complete. The wind-and-canvas sailors laughed at what looked to them like an enormous stone-age canoe. Robert's boat, 150 feet long and only 13 feet wide, presented a snakelike appearance as it was towed from the Brownne Shipyard to Paulus Hook ferry on the Hudson River side of New York, where Robert had set up a workshop. He was well satisfied with the boat itself. Now came the difficult task of installing the engine and paddle wheels so that they would work to the best advantage.

As the boiler went in and the smokestack was erected, the Hudson River sailboatmen turned sullen. Some of them were afraid of this weird contraption, and all of them were jealous. If this boat should become a success, what would happen to their sailing packets which for generations had carried the people up and down the Hudson? One night the captain of a sailing ship purposely ran into the steamboat and damaged it. Repairs were made and from then on Robert was forced to hire a watchman to stand guard at night.

While the inventor looked after his boat, his partner, Chancellor Livingston, who had returned from Paris, was busy at Albany, the capital of

New York. A number of years previously the state had given him the exclusive right to operate steamboats in New York waters for twenty years provided he built one that ran four miles an hour. While he had not yet produced such a boat, he hoped that he soon would and hence asked the state to give him more time to fulfill the requirements. The state granted his request.

Meanwhile, the partners were low on funds. The boat was costing more than Robert had expected, and it was almost impossible to find anyone else who was willing to put money into a steamboat. "Never did a single word of encouragement or bright hope or warm wish cross my path," Robert remembered later. Many people considered him a peculiar, if not crazy, inventor. But he had managed to scrape along before with little help, and somehow the partners were able to do so now. The extra money was found and the *North River Steamboat*, as it was then called, was finished.

If it was strange looking before the engine was put in, it was unbelievably strange afterward. The deck was flat almost from stem to stern. The boiler was in full view, and there was a funny-looking chimney or smokestack amidships. The engine, too, was in plain sight, as were the paddle wheels, which were hung over the side and connected by a shaft. But to Robert this steamboat was a thing of beauty, and he could hardly wait to test it.

He made his first trial run on August 9th, exactly four years after the voyage of his first steamboat in France. Early on the morning of that day he started the fire. By noon steam was up and every part of the machinery was in order. Now the throttle was opened, and the boat began to move out of her berth. A black column of

The Clermont

smoke poured from her stack while a hundred
pairs of eyes looked on in amazement from
neighboring buildings and piers. Robert steamed
up the river for a mile, easily passing all the sailboats, and then stopped to try different numbers

of blades in the paddle wheels. When he was satisfied, he eased the boat back into its slip.

During the next few days he made final adjustments in preparation for the maiden voyage to Albany on August 17th. The trip would be 150 miles long and there were going to be a number of passengers—friends and relatives of Chancellor Livingston who were important people high in society. Monday, August 17th, and the days immediately following would either be the greatest of his life or the most dismal. If the boat succeeded in reaching Albany, he too would reach his own goal. If not—if something broke down—well, he could not spend time thinking about that.

On the famous day Robert was up at dawn going over the engine as he had done a hundred times before. Soon the crew was on board and the engineer touched off the kindling wood in the boiler. By mid-morning the firebox, fed with chunks of wood from the enormous pile on deck, glowed orange with a roaring fire. Wisps of steam issued from the many valves and pipes. Although he did not show it, Robert was tense with excitement as he gave his crew their final instructions.

Shortly before noon the passengers began to arrive, threading their way through the crowd which thronged the approaches to the pier. The passengers were all dressed in finery, looking as if they had stepped out of their drawing rooms or their carriages on a pleasant Sunday afternoon. The ladies were wearing bonnets and the most fragile gowns, while the men appeared in starched ruffles and waistcoats, erect and dignified as their position in society demanded. But a spectator said that of all those on board, the son of the Pennsylvania farmer was the handsomest. His "gentle, manly bearing and freedom from embarrassment, his height, somewhat over six feet, his slender yet energetic form and well accommodated dress, his full and curly dark brown hair" distinguished Robert from others in the crowd.

As the passengers came aboard, they looked scared and unhappy. Except for the Chancellor's beautiful niece, who smiled at Robert, not one of them wanted to make the trip. They feared that they were risking not only their lives, but their reputations. Nothing was more humiliating than to be stared at by the noisy crowd on the shore—or, even worse, to be laughed at. But they had been forced into making the trip by Chancellor Livingston, the head of the family, and they had no choice but to make the best of it.

By one o'clock the passengers were all on board, and Robert was moving swiftly about the boat making final preparations to shove off.

Clouds of smoke rolled from the stack, from time to time pouring down on the immaculate white ruffles of the men's shirt fronts, and the ladies' bonnets. The passengers were sour and disgruntled.

"The moment arrived in which the word was to be given for the boat to move," remembered Robert. "My friends were in groups on the deck. There was anxiety mixed with fear among them. They were silent, sad and weary. I read in their looks nothing but disaster, and almost repented my efforts."

The signal was now given. The lines were cast off, and the chief engineer opened a valve that set the ponderous engine in motion. The boat moved away from the dock and out into the river. Suddenly the engine wheezed to a stop, and the boat swung around in the tide. A look of consternation appeared on the faces of the passengers.

Robert climbed to a platform and addressed the passengers

"There!" said one of them. "I told you so!"

"What a pack of fools we are!" said another.

"A ridiculous scheme! I wish we were well out of it," exclaimed a third. Hearing these remarks and seeing the mutinous looks on the faces of his passengers, Robert climbed to a platform and raised his hand.

"Ladies and gentlemen," he said. "Frankly I do not know what is wrong with the machinery. But if you will give me half an hour, I will find the difficulty, and we will either continue or postpone the trip for the time being." No one raised any objection—at least aloud—and Robert and the engineer quickly went over the machinery. The trouble turned out to be only a minor adjustment, which was quickly made. Immediately thereafter the wheels began to turn again. The prow of the boat swung about to resume its course toward the north.

The sound of clapping and whistling could now clearly be heard from the crowd on shore and as the steamboat gained momentum, the look of fear on the faces of the passengers gave way to utter astonishment. They could not believe that they were moving upstream against the wind. Yet at their very feet the engine chugged reassuringly, and the paddle wheels splashed the water with a steady rhythm, while in the distance to the right, they could see the shoreline of New York drifting past them.

Five—ten—twenty—forty minutes elapsed. The steamboat had left the city far behind and was seeking its way north along the silver river between rugged cliffs that rose sharply on each side. The passengers had lost their fear. Amazement at their progress had given way to enthusiasm and then to congenial high spirits. Now a group in the stern of the boat began to sing. No tribute could have meant more to Robert, for their voices were joined in the Scottish strains of his favorite song:

> *Ye banks and braes o' bonny Doon*
> *How can ye bloom sae fresh and fair;*
> *How can ye chant, ye little birds,*
> *And I sae weary fu' of care?*

If there were tears in Robert's eyes, who could blame him? The years of bitter defeat and of sacrifice had served only to make this journey the more triumphant.

Harriet Livingston, the niece of the Chancellor, was smiling at him. Only if he succeeded with this boat could he, a Pennsylvania farmer's son, expect to marry this beautiful girl. Sometime before, he had finally summoned the courage to ask the Chancellor: "Would you think me too

The passing hours found the steamboat chugging smoothly up the Hudson

bold if I should ask for the hand of Miss Harriet Livingston?"

The Chancellor, after thinking a few moments, had replied: "By no means! Her father may object because you are a humble and poor inventor, and the family may object, but if Harriet does not object—and she seems to have a world of sense— go ahead and my best wishes and blessing go with you."

Now in the first long journey of his steamboat, Robert had so much at stake! With all the attention of a doctor watching over a very sick patient, Robert listened to the heavy breathing of the boiler and to the engine as it labored with its burden.

The passing hours found the steamboat chugging smoothly up the Hudson, now in the heart of a grand and sometimes lonely country. Only occasionally were villages to be seen, clustered on the shore around the sailboat landings. The course of the river led through gorges whose awesome cliffs rose hundreds of feet on each side. Here and there silent forests pressed down to the river bank and the only sounds to be heard, other than the puffing of the engine and the splash of the paddle wheels, were the wailing of sea gulls or the calling of a solitary crane.

As the shadows lengthened and the river took on the soft colors of an evening sky, the shores became misty and indistinct. Soon the boat and its passengers were alone with the river. Only the bright embers from the smokestack and the occasional glow of the firebox relieved the darkness, making weird, shifting patterns in the water and among the trees along the shore. The passengers, tired out from excitement, but contented, bedded down for the night, the gentlemen on deck and the ladies below in the cabin.

But along the shores of the river few were sleeping. Horseback riders had traveled from farmhouse to farmhouse and from town to town with the alarming news that "the devil in a saw-mill is on his way upriver!" Here and there, in the middle of the night, groups gathered along the shores to watch this strange specter, snorting fire, as it appeared from the south and disappeared slowly to the north. Above the river on isolated hill farms, where news of the steamboat had not reached, whole families looked on in terror. Some, believing this was the end of the world, ran deep into the woods for cover.

Morning found the engine of the steamboat still chugging along eighty-five miles north of New York City. Many of the passengers were up with the sun, for there was much excitement to be seen along the banks. By now, the whole valley of the Hudson knew of the progress of

Fulton's boat. All those who could make their way to the wharves of a village, or to the bluffs overlooking the river, were shouting and waving their handkerchiefs.

At one o'clock in the afternoon, Chancellor Livingston's estate, Clermont—from which the steamboat later received its name—loomed in the distance among the trees on the right bank of the river. The Chancellor climbed to the highest point of the deck and waved the passengers to silence.

"Ladies and gentlemen," he said. "You have taken part in what will become one of the great events of history. Since leaving New York you have journeyed 110 miles by steamboat! No such trip has ever before been accomplished or even attempted!" The ring of applause cut off the Chancellor's remarks. He signaled again for silence. "Robert," he commanded, "come up here!" All eyes were turned on the inventor as he climbed to the platform and with quiet modesty took his place beside Livingston.

"This young man," said the Chancellor, "has succeeded in a task that has been so difficult that it has beggered and ruined a score of others who have tried to accomplish it. It is the most notable achievement of our generation. I predict that before the close of the present century ships will be going to Europe under steam! I am happy that I have had a part in the building of this boat. But here is the gentleman who deserves your respect, for his name will go down in history as a benefactor to humanity. This proud vessel is genuinely the fruit of one man's labor—that of Robert Fulton!"

A long round of applause, mixed with cheers, greeted Robert's ears. "Wait," said the Chancellor, "I have not finished! What moment could be more appropriate than this to announce—and I take the greatest pleasure and pride in doing so—the engagement of my niece, Miss Harriet Livingston, to Mr. Robert Fulton!" A second burst of applause echoed across the water. Quite overpowered by this, the greatest moment of his life, Robert could merely stand and smile. He could say nothing. According to one of the passengers, his face was "glorious with love and genius."

The *Clermont* was now directly abreast of the Chancellor's estate. When the weary engine was shut down, the anchor was dropped at once, before the long vessel grounded in shallow water. All of the passengers now went ashore in small boats to pass the night at the Chancellor's manor house.

The next morning they arose early and returned to the *Clermont* for the last part of the journey. At nine o'clock the anchor was hauled aboard, and the wheels once more began to turn. At five in the afternoon the steamboat reached Albany where a large crowd cheered it to a landing.

The most famous steamboat voyage in history had ended.

11

"WILL THEE RISK
THY LIFE?"

MR. BARLOW HAD NOT BEEN PRESENT ON THE
Clermont so Robert described the historic voyage in a long letter. He said that they had gone
150 miles in thirty-two hours against a light
wind, and had passed schooners and sloops as if
they had been anchored. When they had left
New York, he estimated that there were not
thirty people in the whole city who believed that
the boat would travel one mile an hour. "While
we were putting off from the wharf, which was
crowded with spectators," he wrote, "I heard a
number of sarcastic remarks."

In the same letter Robert predicted that the steamboat "will give a cheap and quick conveyance to merchandise on the Mississippi, Missouri and other great rivers, which are now laying open their treasures to . . . our countrymen."

Seeing is believing, and great numbers of people had glimpsed the boat on its way up the Hudson. But despite his confidence, Robert knew that even yet the *Clermont* had not proved itself. Many people felt that while the boat had succeeded in reaching Albany once, it might not be able to do so again. One reason was that in those times the attitude toward inventions was quite different from what it is now. Today we seize upon every new idea with enthusiasm, but then people looked upon inventions with distrust. We must remember that the passengers on the first trip were guests who had more or less been ordered by Chancellor Livingston to make the trip.

The question was, would the public be willing
to pay seven dollars, the agreed price, to go to
Albany by steamboat?

Nearly a month passed before the *Clermont*
was ready to make her first public trip, on September 4, 1807. Fortunately a Quaker named
John Q. Wilson, who was on board that day,
wrote down his recollections, or else we would
never have known much about it.

When Wilson announced that he had decided
to make the trip, a friend exclaimed: "John, will
thee risk thy life in such a concern? I tell thee
she is the most fearful *wild fowl* living, and thy
father ought to restrain thee!" Making his way
to the wharf early on Friday, September 4th,
Wilson found that every pier, street, window and
housetop within sight of the *Clermont* was filled
with spectators. The boat was ready to go. Black
smoke was pouring out of the chimney and

"steam hissed from every ill-fated valve and crevice of the engine." The steersman was standing at the tiller in the stern, just behind the entrance to the ladies' cabin.

Robert Fulton was there, said Wilson. "His remarkably clear and sharp voice was heard above the hum of the multitude and the noise of the engine. All of his actions were confident and decided, unheeding the fearfulness of some, and the doubts and sarcasms of the others."

When the time came to start, there was a delay, just as there had been on the maiden voyage. Quite a number of passengers were on board, and they all looked disturbed. Then Robert announced: "Gentlemen, you need not be uneasy; you shall be in Albany before twelve o'clock tomorrow."

At length, when everything was ready, the engine was started. "The boat moved steadily,

Newburgh residents cheered the passing steamboat

but slowly from the wharf," Wilson recalled. "As she turned up the river there arose such a huzza as ten thousand throats never gave before."

All went well. At Haverstraw Bay there was a man waiting in a skiff who asked if he could come aboard the *Clermont*. Robert ordered a line to be thrown to him, and he was brought alongside. He turned out to be an ignorant fellow who worked in a mill. Somebody had told him that the *Clermont* was a gristmill and on coming aboard he said he "did not know much about a mill going upstream, and came to inquire about it."

There was an Irishman aboard who, seeing a chance to have some fun, showed the miller the *Clermont's* engine. Pleased at this, the miller said: "Now I would like to see the millstones."

"Oh," said the Irishman, "that is a secret which the master," he pointed to Robert, "has not told us yet; but when we come back from Albany with a load of corn, then if you come on board you will see the meal fly."

When the *Clermont* reached West Point, all of the military cadets were waiting on the bluff, and as she steamed passed they cheered heartily. To the steamboat passengers it seemed as if the

entire village of Newburgh and most of Orange
County had turned out, for the whole hillside,
sloping to the water, was covered with people.
The bay was filled with small sailing vessels tack-
ing to and fro in welcome, and the ferryboat
from Fishkill was filled with ladies.

Reaching Albany on schedule, the *Clermont*
took on another load of passengers for her trip
back to New York. She returned without mis-
hap, and when the money was counted, Robert
found that she had made a profit! During the
coming weeks more and more people ventured to
go to Albany by steamboat, thus avoiding a rough
land journey by stagecoach, and a very slow one
by sailing schooner. By late fall, when cold
weather drove her into her slip for the winter,
the future of steamboating on American water-
ways was assured.

The moment that the *Clermont* withdrew from

service for the season, Robert began to tear her apart. He put in new knees and timbers, new deck beams, new deck, windows and cabins and a new boiler. The following spring when she went back on the river, she was practically a new boat, much wider and safer than she had been before. And she was far more elegant. There were now three cabins containing fifty-four berths, a kitchen, dining room and bar, and Robert had fitted up the interior with ornamental paintings, gilding and polished woods. These improvements attracted more passengers. The *Clermont* shortly became a fixture on the Hudson, and she began to pay handsome profits.

Meanwhile Robert started to make plans for the building of boats on Lake Champlain, Long Island Sound and the Mississippi River. The shipyards were soon merry with the clatter of hammers and saws, and the iron foundries with the clang of heavy hammers. The long, colorful era of the side-wheel steamboat had begun.

12

A RACE WITH THE HOPE

IF YOU HAVE EVER FISHED IN SHALLOW WATER where you, as well as the fish, could see your bait, you have made a study of group behavior. The first bold scout—a perch, let us say—swims warily up and looks at the worm. Backing off, he returns again to examine it from a different angle. Finally he takes a bite out of it. At this point a number of other perch, who have been waiting cautiously in the background, dart forth and clean the hook before the first perch has another chance at it.

Unfortunately that is often the way with human beings. When Robert was building the

Clermont and needed more money to finish it, no one would help him. People scorned him and even sought to damage the boat. But when it proved a success, other inventors and business-men—like the timid perch—rushed in to build steamboats and take the business away from Robert and Chancellor Livingston.

One of the men who became a competitor was the Chancellor's own brother-in-law, an inventor named John Stevens. Although he had been interested in steamboats for a number of years, and had built some, they had not been successful. When more money was needed to finish the *Clermont*, Robert and the Chancellor had offered to take Stevens in as a partner, but he had haughtily refused. He said that the *Clermont* would never run because it wasn't well designed.

About the time that the *Clermont* had steamed jauntily up the Hudson, Stevens succeeded in building a boat that was very much the same. He now went to Robert and the Chancellor and told them that he was building a boat that was going to be much faster than the *Clermont*. If they didn't take him in as a partner, he said he would complete his boat, put it into competition with the *Clermont* and ruin their business. Although Robert's invention was protected by law, he and the Chancellor did not care to become mixed up in a family squabble, so they offered Stevens a one-fifth share in the *Clermont*.

Because they refused to give him the credit for inventing the steamboat, Stevens decided not to accept this second offer. Instead he finished the boat he was building, which he called the *Phoenix*, and started running it right under the noses of the partners. They decided that they must fight, and fight they did. At length they succeeded in having the *Phoenix* tied up. This, however, did not discourage Stevens. He merely sent his boat down the Atlantic coast to the Delaware River and started running it there.

Meanwhile he built a "horseboat" and began operating that in competition with Robert and the Chancellor. This vessel was really two boats harnessed together, with a paddle wheel revolving in the space between them. But instead of a steam engine turning the wheel, Stevens had built a treadmill on deck, which was propelled by two horses. It was not a "steamboat," and therefore the partners could do nothing about it.

As time went on, it became clear that there was apparently nothing Stevens would not resort to. "I have just been informed," Robert wrote him in 1812, "that your foreman has been trying to get some of my workmen to go to work for you at Hoboken. I hope this is not true. But if it is and one man moves from my shop, I will insist on all the rights to which I am entitled."

Stevens replied that the letter was an insult. He wanted to know what "rights" Robert was talking about. He said he had no knowledge of the matter about the workmen, and that anyway Robert's threat would never have any influence on what he did. In answer, Robert repeated the charge that someone from Stevens' shop was trying to hire his men away, and he had been told that Stevens knew all about it. Robert then went on to describe his "rights."

"You are running a steamboat without a license from my partner and me, and you are carrying horses, gigs, carriages and cattle in contempt of my United States patent. In your letters last winter you claimed yourself as the inventor of steamboats, and I was a mere cipher.

138

"You have never had any claims on me, either as a relation or a friend, yet we came forward twice and offered you an interest in our business. But because you want to be thought of as the inventor of the steamboat, you have waged constant war with Livingston and Fulton." Finally Robert told Stevens that he was through writing or talking on the subject. From now on he would answer Stevens in the law courts.

The partners finally managed to keep Stevens in check, but they found that preventing other opposition boats from sprouting on the river was like trying to slay that ancient nine-headed water serpent, Hydra, which could grow two heads as fast as one was cut off. In 1811 Robert said he was spending most of his time trying to defeat twenty-two "pirates" who had banded together and stolen some of his workmen to build a boat called the *Hope*. Later, steaming brazenly up and

The engineers were stoking their furnaces

down the river between Albany and New York,
the captain of the *Hope* even dared the captain
of the *Clermont* to race him.

On July 27, 1811, both boats were at their
piers in Albany preparing for the first steamboat
race in history. The engineers were stoking their

The CLERMONT *raced the* HOPE *in the first steam-boat race in history*

furnaces with dry pine wood which blazed fright-
fully, sending a storm of sparks into the air from
their smokestacks. Suddenly, before the *Clermont*
was ready, the *Hope* started out from its pier into
the channel. Anxiously viewing the head start of
the *Hope*, the *Clermont's* captain spurred his
engineer to greater effort. A few precious moments later he turned the valve. Steam poured
into the cylinder; the clanking bell-cranks strained
against the fly wheel and the paddles began to
thrash the water. The *Clermont* moved quickly
into the channel directly behind her adversary.

As the *Clermont* tried to pass the *Hope*, the
people on shore, feverish with excitement, jumped
up and down and shouted. But the *Hope* hugged
the middle of the channel. Try as he would, the
captain of the *Clermont* could not seem to get
by. For many miles down the river the two boats
struggled to gain still more speed. Seeking to

raise the pressure of their boilers, the engineers ordered more pine logs thrown in, until their fireboxes became roaring infernos. The machinery trembled as it strained to turn the paddle wheels faster.

About two miles above the town of Hudson the engineer of the *Clermont* was able to get a few more revolutions per minute out of his engine, and the captain swung out of the channel to pass the *Hope*. Inch by inch the *Clermont* began to gain. The people on board were wild with excitement. They shouted and shook their fists at each other across the narrow interval of water that separated the two boats. Steadily but slowly the *Clermont* overtook the *Hope*, its paddle wheels beating the water to a lather. Now the race was even. As the desperate captain of the *Hope* called to his engineer for more steam, the *Clermont* began to pull ahead.

Suddenly the stretch of water between the two boats lessened. A hundred voices shouted in alarm, but it was too late. The two boats came together with a sickening crash. The engineers grabbed the throttles, the wheels ceased to turn, and the wounded steamboats drifted to a stop. As they viewed the damage, their tempers flared. The two captains, white with anger, called the race off and the boats limped on down the river to New York.

That fall Robert at last succeeded in having the outlaw boat tied up, together with another called the *Perseverance*. Once more the river belonged to the *Clermont* and another Fulton boat called the *Car of Neptune*. Never had Robert felt more exhausted. He was no longer merely an inventor. Now, as builder, operator and protector of his steamboats, he had to be a construction superintendent, businessman and policeman.

13

CONQUERING
THE MISSISSIPPI

A MAN STARTING ONE STEAMBOAT LINE HAD
all he could do. In starting a number of lines at
the same time, Robert was awash with his heavy
burden, but he was not going to be satisfied until
he had steamboats running on every waterway
in the country. His most daring venture was to
send an engineer named Nicholas J. Roosevelt
west to build the first steamboat for use on the
Monongahela, Ohio, and Mississippi rivers.

With only a few men and some tools, Roosevelt arrived in Pittsburgh in 1811 to start work.
Today it is hard to imagine the conditions un-

der which he built his boat, the *New Orleans*. He had to take his crew out into the woods and cut down the trees, drag them to the river and float them downstream to the place where they were building their boat. The logs had to be cut into planks. This in itself was a backbreaking task with the primitive saws then in use.

Roosevelt's men had no sooner cut their timber and started work on the hull than a severe rainstorm struck Pennsylvania. The waters of the Monongahela rose rapidly, and soon all their precious piles of lumber were afloat. Much of it sailed downstream. Weeks later, when the river rose a second time, they came very near losing the whole boat.

At last the engine was installed, and the 116-foot *New Orleans* was finished. Roosevelt's plan was to voyage from Pittsburgh down the Monongahela to the Ohio, down the Ohio to the Mississippi and down that broad river to New Orleans. The purpose of this fantastic trip on unknown waters filled with snags, shallows, sand bars, rocks and rapids, was to prove that it was possible to navigate these waters in a steamboat. Of course only Robert Fulton and Nicholas Roosevelt believed it could be done. People were saying that it was one thing to run a steamboat on still water, or through the waves of a lake, but quite another to survive the dangers of a swift-flowing river.

In September, 1811, the *New Orleans* was at last ready to start. Roosevelt had conquered all the troubles of building the boat, but he was now faced with an obstacle that he hadn't foreseen. He needed a crew to man the boat—but nobody wanted to go with him. This did not speak well for all the hardy frontiersmen who had been fighting Indians. Apparently they were willing to risk their lives against bows and arrows and scalping knives, but not against a steam engine. The truth is that not a single scout or trapper answered the call for deck hands. One by one Roosevelt finally managed to recruit the fourteen members of his crew. He had a captain, pilot, engineer, six deck hands and firemen, a cook, waiter, two female servants and a large Newfoundland dog named Tiger. Mrs. Roosevelt insisted on accompanying her husband.

"Imagine allowing a woman to go on a trip like that!" gossiped the people of Pittsburgh. "*I'd* sooner cross the Atlantic in a canoe!"

"When they hit the rapids below Louisville," announced an old raftsman who knew the river, "there'll be nothing left but kindling wood!"

Like Robert Fulton, Roosevelt had learned to ignore these prophets of doom, and his wife was no more concerned than he. Early on the September morning that the boat was to leave, she was happily settled on board, tending to all kinds of housekeeping chores for her crew of fourteen.

As the hour of sailing approached, the usual crowd of wide-eyed unbelievers and hecklers lined the shore. Presently the lines were cast off, and the *New Orleans* moved grandly away from the dock, paddled into the river channel and downstream out of sight.

Eager with thoughts of adventure beyond every twist and bend of the river, the crew spent most of the first day on deck. A pageant of scenery, wild and grand, unfolded on both sides of the river. Upon the approach of the steamboat, animals scurried for cover into the unbroken forests. Large birds took to their wings from the shallow waters near the shores. Especially when the shadows of evening veiled the river, and the stars shone, did it seem as if they were somehow journeying through a different world. The friendly chugging of the engine, the splash of the paddle wheels, and the ripple of water along the sides of the boat were the only sounds to be heard.

When it became so dark that Mr. Jack, the pilot, could no longer see, he steered to a spot where the river bank dropped into deep water. Then the deck hands tied the boat securely to the trees at the water's edge. The fire in the boiler turned to embers, and the hiss of steam died down to a whisper. On the edge of the wilderness the crew of the *New Orleans* slept.

Early the next morning the wheels were turning again, and the members of the crew were once more on deck to see and hear the strange views and sounds of the new country through which the river flowed. Excited, they returned the greetings of all the people of a small river town who had gathered on the bank to watch the steamboat pass. On the second day the *New Orleans* steamed into Cincinnati, where it paused while the deck hands brought on board a new supply of firewood. Then it was off again, to the wonder of the settlers, who had never seen a steamboat. So the days passed.

On October first, after a long day's journey, the *New Orleans* reached Louisville after dark. When in the light of a full moon the people saw the flames and sparks from the smokestack and the cloud of steam pouring from the safety valve, many of them were terrified. Some thought it was the end of the world. Others were sure that the blazing comet of 1811 had fallen into the Ohio River. All of them were amazed that the *New Orleans* had come from as far away as it had. Roosevelt was looked upon as a hero, and the people of Louisville held a public dinner in his honor when he arrived there.

of fact, Roosevelt was none too sure of it himself. It was a dry season. The water in the river was low, and the rocks under the rapids were very near the surface. At length he decided that they would have to stand by until there was a heavy rain. He hoped that this would raise the height of the river sufficiently to carry the *New Orleans* safely through the rapids.

While they waited, Mrs. Roosevelt gave birth to a child, who became the youngest steamboat passenger in history. At last in November, heavy rains fell. The Ohio rose rapidly, and Roosevelt announced that they must leave at once, since he calculated that the depth in the shallowest part of the rapids was now five inches more than that required by the boat.

Accordingly a roaring fire was built in the boiler to assure the greatest possible pressure of steam. Everything on deck was tied down. While

154

an awe-struck crowd watched, Roosevelt gave the crew their final instructions. Then, as steam shrieked from the safety valve, the *New Orleans* ploughed into the channel and headed downstream toward the falls. As the boat began to gain speed in the swollen waters, the crew stood grim-faced at their stations. Tiger, the Newfoundland dog, sensing danger, crouched tensely at Mrs. Roosevelt's feet. Faster, faster, the river current pulled the *New Orleans* onward. As it reached the headwaters of the falls, it began to rock and roll.

Now all eyes were fastened on Mr. Jack, the pilot, as he signaled the helmsman from his lookout in the bow. In a few moments the boat plunged into the rapids. On all sides angry gray water billowed over the rocks. Spray dashed over the deck. The boat plunged and arose, rolled and trembled. Steam roared from the safety valve.

The NEW ORLEANS *hurtled down the rapids of the Mississippi*

The *New Orleans* hurtled down its frothy course, vaulted into the quiet water below the falls, recovered her equilibrium, and stopped, as the engineer shut off the steam. It was all over and they were safe! With gratitude to the Almighty, Roosevelt ordered the men to drop anchor for a while here before continuing their journey.

While they were still resting after their trial, the boat, although at anchor, began to stagger and sway as if it had struck bottom. The crew looked at each other in consternation. The dog began to whine and growl. The swaying continued for a few moments, then stopped as quickly as it had begun. No one could explain what had caused it. An examination of the boat proved that there was nothing wrong there.

In the middle of the night the lurching and swaying began again, and the crew grew fearful and started to feel sick. Still, no one could imagine

The boat began to lurch and sway

what was happening. While the journey continued the following morning, everyone on board was silent, as if expecting some great disaster. The next few days were frightful for the *New Orleans* and her crew. The broad Mississippi, which they had now reached, was not the river that Mr. Jack, the pilot, had known. It appeared to be in the grip of a flood, and he had no idea where the channel was.

At New Madrid, Missouri, the voyagers learned that they had been through a terrible earthquake. The land had been wrenched apart, and a huge chasm had swallowed up some of the houses. Many of the people begged to be taken on board the *New Orleans*, which seemed safer than the land. Others, seeing the boat's pillar of smoke and cloud of steam, thought it had something to do with the earthquake and were even more afraid than before. On board the *New Orleans*, it was reported that:

> No one seemed disposed to talk, and when there was any conversation, it was carried on in whispers almost. Tiger, who appeared, alone, to be aware of the earthquake while the vessel was in motion, prowled about, moaning and growling, and when he came

159

and placed his head on Mrs. Roosevelt's lap, it was a sure sign of a commotion of more than usual violence. Orders were given in low tones; and the usual cheerful "aye, aye, sir" of the sailors was almost inaudible. . . .

The steamboat continued downriver, although the crew was worn out from lack of rest. When they tied up along the bank at night, the crash of huge trees falling into the water around their mooring made sleep impossible. Nothing seemed secure. One evening, rather than tie up to the bank, they chose to make the boat fast at the foot of an island in the middle of the river. This seemed much safer. Hopeful of a good night's sleep the crew tumbled into their bunks. But in the middle of the night the boat began to shake again, and they heard a kind of bumping and scraping outside.

At daylight they were dumbfounded to find

that the island had gone! Apparently it had broken up and sunk. The tree to which they had moored the boat had disappeared beneath the water, and the hawser was still tied to it. It was necessary to cut the rope with an axe. This was all most terrifying. Mrs. Roosevelt recalled that she could not do anything—sleep, read, or sew. Half the time Mr. Jack had no idea where he was steering the boat, since in many places the river had left its old channel and was now flowing through what had been a forest. At times the *New Orleans* had to thread its way through the trees. In the half light of the forest, canoes filled with hostile Indians would appear and disappear, adding to the voyagers' worries.

The Indians had received word that the *Penelore*, or fire canoe, as they called the *New Orleans*, was on its way downriver. To them the comet of 1811, the earthquake and the fire canoe were all one. The sparks from the chimney and the tail of the comet were the same, as were the rumbling of the paddle wheels and the shaking of the ground.

One day, a canoe full of Indians darted out of the woods and streaked through the water toward the *New Orleans*. As the Indians whooped, the engineer opened his throttle wide and the paddle wheels turned at top speed. The canoe gradually fell behind. That night Roosevelt heard a commotion on deck which he thought was an attack by the redskins. When he rushed above, he found that the cabin was on fire. All hands rallied and managed to put it out. However, it had not been set by the Indians—someone had simply stacked the wood too close to the stove.

The *New Orleans* survived every catastrophe. Finally emerging from the earthquake zone it

A canoe full of Indians streaked toward the
NEW ORLEANS

steamed into the pleasant reaches of the lower Mississippi. On the peaceful last days of the trip the deck hands, who had had more adventure than they had bargained for, were glad to relax. At Natchez, they received a glorious welcome. A few days later an even greater celebration awaited the boat at the city for which she was named.

The *New Orleans* had reached her destination, and the age of the steamboat had come to the Mississippi.

14

A MAN TO REMEMBER

BENJAMIN WEST, THE ARTIST WHO HAD BEEN Robert Fulton's teacher in London twenty-six years before, received a letter in 1813. In it he learned that his former pupil had fourteen steamboats running in America on lakes, rivers and bays from the Canadian border to New Orleans. "And I am building thirteen (more) for various waters," Robert announced proudly.

Now he had plans for building steamboats on the Ganges River in India and was talking of a fleet of side-wheelers for Russia. For many years he had been urging that the Erie Canal be built. He was now a member of the committee to draw up plans for that great man-made waterway. In 1811 he wrote Chancellor Livingston that he had also been doing a lot of thinking about the possibility of steam railroads.

When the United States found itself in a second war with Great Britain in 1812, Robert eagerly went back to work on his submarine and his torpedoes. He drew up a plan for the world's first battleship. Early in 1814 the government commissioned him to go ahead and build it. In a colorful ceremony this heavy craft, 167 feet long and 56 feet wide, was launched on October 29, 1814. She carried two 100-pound cannons in the bow and had thirty-two portholes in her sides through which as many guns could fire red-hot shot. She was equipped with a huge steam pump and hose that could throw powerful jets of water onto the decks of enemy ships, washing their sailors overboard and soaking their guns.

This battleship, *Fulton the First*, was built to protect New York harbor from the British. As soon as it was launched, Robert went to work to install its mighty steam engine. Hearing of this dreadnaught the British became alarmed and put spies on the inventor's trail, with orders to take him prisoner.

One night British ships in Long Island Sound sent a task force ashore to raid a house where they had learned that Robert was staying. The raid was carried out and the house was sacked, but Robert was not captured. He had planned to be there, but fortunately he had been delayed.

While all these many affairs burdened his days, he did not neglect his family. A dream had come true! After the maiden voyage of the *Clermont* he had married the beautiful Harriet Livingston and had gone to live in a huge house overlooking the river. Here he played with his children and once again took great pleasure in painting. To young and hopeful artists and promising inventors, such as he had once been, he gave large sums of money. And he was glad to build a new barn for his sisters on their farm in Pennsylvania or to present them with expensive cattle.

Because he was a mechanic among mechanics, the men in his shops admired and respected him. "We were always pleased to see him about his shops," remembered one of Robert's workmen. "With his rattan cane in hand, he always appeared to me the counterpart of an English nobleman."

"I have to this day," recalled Robert's chief engineer, "a most distinct and strongly impressed likeness on my mind. He had all the traits of a man with the gentleness of a child. I never heard him use harsh words to any one of those employed under him no matter what they did. And I can remember the times when his labors were so severe. With his waistcoat unbuttoned, he would walk up and down for hours in deep thought, scarcely noticing anything passing him."

In January, 1815, while Robert was installing his battleship's engines, he had to go to New Jersey with his lawyer, a Mr. Emmet. On the way back the two men stopped at Robert's shop and spent three hours looking at boats being re-fitted there. They came out just in time to see the ferry grinding its way through the ice into the slip.

"Come on!" shouted Robert. "We can catch the ferry by taking this short cut across the ice." At a run the two men started off through the cold. Suddenly, with no warning, the ice gave way under Emmet, and he sank into the frigid waters of the Hudson. Robert went after him.

*With great effort Robert pulled Mr. Emmet out
of the water*

Only with the utmost effort was he able to pull his friend out of the water and haul him to safety. Upon reaching home, Robert became very ill.

The doctors ordered him to bed, but when he heard that the men working on the battleship needed him, he arose and dressed and journeyed through the cold all the way to Paulus Hook. This was too much for him. He became desperately sick and lived only until February 23rd.

The courageous events leading to his death—like those of his life—were an inspiration to the people of New York and the country. They honored him as they had never honored any private citizen before.

The legislature of the state of New York announced that it would wear mourning for some weeks. Officials of the state and national government journeyed to New York City, where a silent throng of people lined the streets through which the funeral procession passed. Church bells tolled, and each minute the booming of cannon sounded from the West Battery and from the great steam battleship, *Fulton the First.*

15

THE CLERMONT
SAILS AGAIN

IN 1909, ONE HUNDRED AND TWO YEARS AFTER
the *Clermont* made its historic voyage, the now
great city of New York held a naval celebration
in memory of Henry Hudson, who discovered
the river, and in memory of Robert Fulton, who
introduced steam navigation to it.

Warships from seven nations gathered in a
mighty armada to pay tribute to the man who
had built the first modern battleship. A fleet of
side-wheel steamboats, some of them over 400
feet long and as high as a five-story building,

In 1909 the city of New York honored Robert Fulton and his steamboat

steamed majestically beside the battleships. A thousand flags were flying. From the banks of the Hudson millions of people looked upon this marvelous display.

At the head of the long procession of ships steamed a vessel called the *Clermont*—a faithful copy of Robert Fulton's original boat—its stack sending up clouds of smoke, its engine puffing and its paddle wheels splashing the water. On board were grandchildren and great-grandchildren of those who had taken that first voyage. They were all dressed in their best clothes, just as their ancestors had been in 1807.

The new *Clermont* had not carried them far before they raised their voices in song. It was a Scottish ballad—the favorite of a poor farmer's son who had become one of the world's great inventors:

Ye banks and braes o' bonny Doon
How can ye bloom sae fresh and fair?
How can ye chant, ye little birds
And I sae weary fu' of care?

INDEX

ST. MICHAEL'S SCHOOL,
BRIDGEPORT, CONN.

ST. MICHAEL'S SCHOOL,
BRIDGEPORT, CONN.